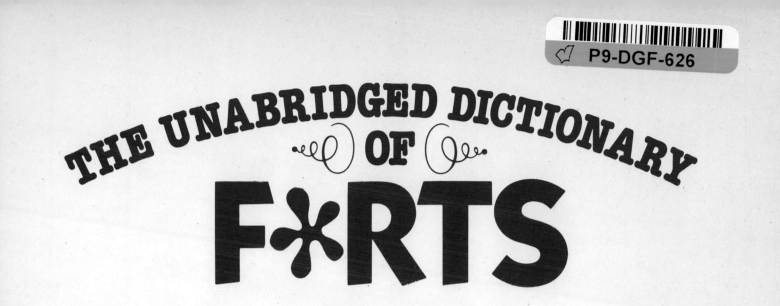

THE UNABRIDGED DICTIONARY OF F*RTS

DONALD WETZEL

CONTEMPORARY BOOKS, INC.

CHICAGO ▪ NEW YORK

Published by Contemporary Books, Inc.
180 North Michigan Avenue, Chicago, Illinois 60601
Manufactured in the United States of America
International Standard Book Number: 0-8092-4884-0

Published simultaneously in Canada by Beaverbooks, Ltd.
195 Allstate Parkway, Valleywood Business Park
Markham, Ontario L3R 4T8 Canada

Introduction

A long time ago—about a year, when I was eleven—I decided to write a book about farts, and I did. Much to my surprise it was actually made into a book.

When I first started doing research on the subject of farts I could not get cooperation from a soul. I would ask a person, "Do you have an intersting fart you would like to talk about?" Or, "Is there any particular fart that is your favorite?" Or "What is the worst fart you can think of?" And you would not believe how people would act. They would back off every time. Like I had asked to see their navel or something. I got no help at all.

So I did it on my own. But once it was actually a book, everything changed. Overnight, everyone I met was a fart expert. All kinds of people, strange and otherwise—even girls—came up to me and said, "Here is a fart you missed, you dummy." Then they would tell me about their dumb fart. All I heard about was farts. New farts, old farts, crazy farts. It was a nuisance.

Well, like my father says, "It is an ill wind that blows no good." So here in this new fart book are all the farts I missed in the first book, and I hope this will be an end of it.

Note

The farts in this book have been arranged alphabetically. This way, if there is a certain fart you are looking for you can go right to it.
  For the purpose of identification, the farts in this book are divided into two groups:

  1. Your farts
  2. Someone else's farts.

This should make things even easier for you.

The **Anarchist Fart**

A

A person who lets lets loose an Anarchist Fart is a person who does not like religion or rich people. He will hold back a fart for hours if he has to just so he can let it go in a bank or a church. In fact the only reason he will go in a church is so that he can fart there. He has to be admired for the way he can hold it back like that and then express himself with a fart, although it really does not seem like a nice thing to do. But he gets away with it. Who knows who farted in church?

The **Anticipated Fart**

Neither sound nor odor are diagnostic in identifying this fart. It is usually identified as a group one fart, although it is not impossible to identify when it is a group two (somebody else's fart). This one warns that it is back there waiting for some time before it arrives. A person who is uneasy for a time in a crowd and who later farts at a time when they think no one will notice has farted an Anticipated Fart. Identification is no problem when you are the farter.

The Autobahn Fart

If you happen to be driving on the autobahn in Germany you will notice signs saying **Ein Fahrt** and **Aus Fahrt**. From these signs you might get the idea that the Germans are being told when to fart and when not to, **Ein Fahrt** meaning you should hold it in, and **Aus Fahrt** meaning you can let it go now. Of course there is often a lot of distance between an **Ein Fahrt** sign and an **Aus Fahrt** sign, and if that is what the signs really meant a lot of Germans would blow themselves up driving along the autobahn. Fortunately what these signs are really telling you is how to get on and off the autobahn.

The Back Seat Fart

B

This is a fart that occurs only in automobiles. If you are in the front seat it is a group two, or somebody else's fart. If you are alone in the back seat it is a group one fart. In either case, of course, it is the same fart. It is identified chiefly by odor, the way some birds are identified mostly by their song, such as your little warblers that stay high up in the trees, or very shy birds of the deep swamp or woods.

I thought I should explain this. Some farts you hear. Some farts you smell. And some can be identified both ways. The back seat fart can usually be concealed by traffic noise as it is eased-out and not very loud. But its foul odor will give it away, due to the way air moves around in a car. And then someone in the front seat will say, who farted in the back seat? Which is silly if there is only one person in the back seat, of course. This is a fairly rare fart due to the restriction of its range or habitat.

The **Barf Fart**

The Barf Fart is to the world of farts what the buzzard is to the world of birds. It is in a class by itself, and not to be envied because of that. For instance, consider the buzzard. How ugly can a bird get? The same with the Barf Fart. How rotten can a fart really be? Or consider again how there are several different birds that eat carrion, but the buzzard is the only bird that will **only** eat carrion; just as there are several different farts that will make other people barf, but the Barf Fart is the only fart that will make the **farter** bart. And there are other similarities, but enough already.

Fortunately this fart is quite rare.

The Barred Owl Fart

A familiarity with owls calls is helpful in identifying this fart. The barred owl or swamp owl is common in parts of Alabama. Almost any morning if you get up just before daybreak you can hear one of these birds talking to himself. Or maybe two of them calling back and forth. Which is not the point. The point is that this call is kind of like a crazy laugh. Particularly the way it ends. An old bird guide we have says it is maniacal. If you hear a fart that has about eight notes in it, ending on a couple of down notes, and it sounds maniacal, you have heard the rare Barred Owl Fart. When you add this one to your life list of identified farts you are really getting some place as a fart expert.

The **Boom-Box Fart**

The distinguishing characteristic that you look for with this fart is the inconsiderate nature of the farter, usually a teenage kid or a man. He may or may not be carrying a boom-box, but he is the sort of person who takes his boom-box to the woods or the beach or the park and plays it as loud as he can, and to hell with everyone else. The same sort of person who leaves disposable diapers on picnic tables. This is a deliberate, loud, rank, show-off fart in otherwise lovely surroundings. It would be nice if this fart could be eliminated, but I see no way this could be done short of violence.

The **Boomerang Fart**

Who has not been surprised by the tricky Boomerang Fart? What happens is that a person farts a particularly evil sort of fart. It is so bad that the person will quickly walk away from it, into the next room, or around a corner of the house if he is outside, and he will think, "Phew, thank goodness I got away from that one." And just about then it will hit him again, with every bit as powerful a stink as it had when launched.

    This is a really lousy fart for a person if he is alone when he farts and then goes and joins a bunch of people. What can he say? That he farted way back in the next room? Who would believe him?

The **Boreal Fart**

This is a windy fart that happens to be cold. You may not know what Boreal means, but you will know the fart.
(Boreal is an adjective and means of, or pertaining to, the North wind. I looked it up. And that's what I thought it meant.)
You will recognize this fart immediately, a group one identification, as it is the only fart that blows cold. "My," you will think, "what a strange fart." Just remember the name, Boreal. Rare.

The **Broccoli Fart**

Identification of this fart is by odor alone. It smells like broccoli cooking. If you have nothing against broccoli this can be one of the nicer farts. If it is a group one fart and you have, as a matter of fact, been eating broccoli, then you have a True Broccoli Fart (look under T) which is really not rare at all.

C

Any fart that makes you laugh even when you are alone is probably a Comic Fart. This is a fart that seems to be trying to make you laugh, usually by making all kinds of crazy sqealing sounds or imitating human speech or barking like a dog. It is no ordinary fart and you know it. It is a real joker. Regrettably, the Comic Fart—the real thing—seems only to occur when you are alone, when there is no one else to enjoy it. You may even think at the time, "What a pity the gang missed that one."

The **Common Fart**

This fart needs little description. It is to the world of farts what the house sparrow is to the world of birds. It has no particularly distinguishing characteristics except its commonness. As the house sparrow is the bird you see when there are no other birds around, the Common Fart is the one fart you are sure to run across at least once each day, group one or group two identification, sometime between sunup and sundown. I can see no point in describing this fart any further.

The **Dead Rat Fart**

This is an awful name for a fart by a lady, but there is a reason for it. It is called that only to spare the lady embarrassment. What happens is you walk up to receptionist somewhere and she is all alone at her desk—there is no one within fifty feet of her, so you know it had to be her—and there is an odor so vile you cannot believe it. And you know immediately that you must do something to help the situation, so you say, "Wow, lady, there must be a dead rat around here." This gives her a chance to nod and look around and say something like, "Yes, isn't it terrible. I am told it will be taken care of soon." After that, with some luck, you and the receptionist should get along fine.

The Dog Whistle Fart

This is a fart that only a dog can hear. A very high frequency fart. You didn't hear it yourself, but you have farted a good one. Unfortunately, the dumb dog thinks you are calling him. He gets all to attention. Nobody else has heard a thing, but by the time they begin to smell something and are wondering who did it, the stupid dog has come up to you and stands there wagging his tail or maybe even offering to shake hands, if that is a trick he knows. Of course, the other people know it must have been you who farted. This one's a real fluke, of course.

The **Drunk Fart**

There are some times when a drunk can be pretty funny, but not when they are farting. A real drunk has no sense at all in this matter. He may not even know he is farting. Generally, the Drunk Fart is a long drawn-out, sometimes undulating, fart, He just lets it roll. You can tell that he doesn't care about a thing. It is surely one of the most gross farts there is, but it may help if you try to think of it as simply a cry for help. This may be hard to do, however.

The Dud Fart

As a matter of fact the Dud Fart, as the name might make you think, is not really a fart at all. It is a fart that fails. For this reason it is strictly a group one identification fart, because there is no real way you can identify a fart that somebody else expected to fart but didn't. It is the most private of all farts. Only the farter knows what happened. What happened was he didn't fart. At all. This can be seen as a good thing or a bad thing, depending on the circumstances. Still, it is my opinion that in most cases the farter usually feels a little disappointed. As when you answer the phone and it is a wrong number. This fart is about as common as wrong number calls and as easy to identify.

E

This is a fart that can be wrongly identified if you jump to conclusions because of its name. It is not some great loud fart in an empty gym or on the rim of the Grand Canyon or something like that where there might actually be an echo. The true Echo Fart is a fart that makes its own echo. It is a two-toned fart, the first tone loud, then a pause, and then second tone, faint. Like an echo. This is the only real Echo Fart, and it is as rare as lots of other farts many times fancier. Just remember that real thing is one hundred percent fart, and you will not be fooled.

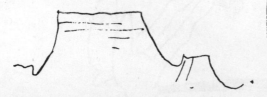

The Five-Finger Gag Fart

Even more sickening than the Sweet Fart. (Look under S.) The odor is indescribable it is so rotten. If you identify this one as a group one fart you would be smart to go and see a doctor. You are sick.

A real easy group one identification. You are driving along on the freeway and you fart. However, the real trick is to catch the Freeway Fart as a group two indentification. So I know it can be done. I have done it. But you have to watch the drivers ahead of you very carefully for the signs.

Usually they first take a quick look in the rear view mirror and speed the car up some. I don't know why they do this, but they do. Then they will pretend to stretch. They can make quite a show of it. They will twist around sometimes in a way that can be alarming. But what they are doing, they are getting ready to fart. Then they fart.

You can tell when it is over because they slow down again. Sometimes they look around at the scenery or even wave at another car. I guess they think they have been pretty tricky. But so have you, if you have caught them at it. This fart is about as common as you can get.

The **Galumpher Fart**

G

This is a fart by a fellow with a low forehead and very large hands. He will fart and then smell his index finger. No one knows why. Probably he is just confused.

The **Gemini Fart**

If you are a Gemini and you fart a fart that
seems to you especially novel or
creative, or which, in your opinion,
is a pretty sensitive sort of a fart,
you have farted without a doubt the
very special Gemini Fart. Which, if you
are heavy into astrology, should make
you very happy.

The Girdle Fart

You may wonder how a young male kid like myself has come to know all about the Girdle Fart, but that is neither here nor there. The Girdle Fart is a fart by a lady wearing a girdle. To be honest it is in my opinion one of the most interesting as well as possibly the funniest fart I have ever heard of. What happens—and I am quoting here—is that the lady farts in her girdle and the fart rolls slowly up and finally comes out up near her back somewhere. If the girdle is a real tight one, or if the lady is a fat lady, sometimes the fart doesn't get out at all. It just rolls around like a marble. If this is not a funny fart, I have never heard of one. To get one of these on your list you would have to get awfully friendly with some girdle-wearing lady or other, it seems to me. Or be one yourself. Rare.

The **Goose Fart**

This is not a bird fart, although I guess you could call it a foul fart sometimes. (That was a pun.) Actually, the goose I am talking about here is the kind where you get goosed. That is what is most clearly diagnostic about the Goose Fart. It has a recoil factor that can make you feel as though you have not just farted, you have somehow goosed yourself. This is one of the more explosive farts, which is why you get the recoil effect, I guess. You will know it when it happens to you, no question about it.

The **Gossamer Fart**

If any fart can be described as lovely this would have to
be the fart, although that may be going a little far, neat as
the Gossamer Fart is. I mean a fart is a fart, after all. But it
is unusually soft and pleasant sounding in tone and with
only the most faint sort of odor, such as vanilla or Milk
Duds or something else nice. You are hardly aware you have released a fart. It is
more like a little butterfly has drifted by or something.

I may be making too much of this. Whatever, if you fart a fart sometime and the
person with you says, "Well, that was cute," you have probably farted the Gossamer
Fart, and the person with you just doesn't want to get emotional about it.

The Gravity Fart

The reason this fart happens when it does—it happens right after you get up from lying down—is because of the force of gravity. You get up, things go down, and out goes the fart. If you stop and think about it, if it was not for the force of gravity we all might be farting through our ears or out the tops of our heads. Thank goodness for gravity.

The Just-When-You-Thought-You-Were-Safe Fart

J

The name of this fart practically says it all. You think that finally you are alone at last, and you let it go. But your friends have forgotten something and here they come back, all of them. Or, look who is here: your girl friend. Surprise! And there is no place to hide. Unfortunately, this is a very common fart.

M

This is a fart by a full-grown man who will look angry and threatening every time he farts. As though he is daring anyone to say something about it. Nobody says anything. Why should they? It was only a fart.

The Malted Milk Ball Fart

Odor alone is diagnostic and positively identifies this fart. It smells exactly like malted milk balls. No other food works this way. It is as rare in its way as is the wood ibis among North American birds, which is the only American stork. Common where found.

The **Moral Majority Fart**

This is a very serious fart. There is nothing funny about it at all. It is like a black cloud. A person will fart a Moral Majority Fart in a room full of people talking and laughing and a silence will come over the room as though someone had thrown a switch. The last thing you would do is laugh at the person who farted such a fart. Mostly you would feel sad for him, because a fart like that just has to hurt.

The **Morning Fart**

Everyone knows this fart. You get up in the morning and are wandering around still only half awake and, BRAP! you fart a real firecracker. "My, my," you think, "where did that come from?"

The Mouse Fart

The distinguishing feature of
the Mouse Fart is how small it is
and how quick. You have seen
a mouse disappear behind a chair
or under a bed so quickly you are
not sure if you really saw a mouse.
The Mouse Fart is like that. It
happens so quick you are not sure
for a minute if you have really
farted. Then you become sure. To
be so small, the Mouse Fart is
surprisingly potent.

The Moxie Fart

This is a very loud and startling
fart by a kid. If there is someone
at least fifty years old around
when it happens they are apt to say, "Kid, you got Moxie." You may not know what
Moxie is—I don't anyhow—but apparently it's okay to have it. This is probably the only
fart by a kid that old people will really think is neat. When you are a kid you never
know when you are going to do something right. Like fart a Moxie Fart.

The **Mustard Fart**

A burning kind of fart much like the Fire Fart (from my previous book), except that this one has a dampness to it, which is where it gets its name. From the color. It is one of the most positively identifiable of all farts, and one of the most gross. This is strictly a group one identification, unless you are in the habit of examining other people's underwear, which I would hope you are not.

The Occult Fart

This rare fart occurs only during a seance. For instance, there is some heavy mumbo jumbo going on but nothing is happening. No one is answering from the Other Side, much as the spirits are being importuned to give a sign. No knocks. No voices. Nothing. And then this ghostly fart. A real boomer! Hollow sounding, but loud. And everyone there swears he or she didn't fart. A sign, at last. It even has an odor. Imagine! And they all go home happy, I suppose.

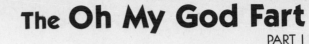

The **Oh My God Fart**

The story of how this most rotten stinking fart got its name is interesting. This is a true story. One rainy day about a year ago I took a hard-boiled egg to school in my lunch. For some reason I put the egg in my raincoat pocket and forgot about it.

I do not much care for hard-boiled eggs.

Then I forgot about the raincoat and left it in the cloakroom.

After about a month the classroom began to have a peculiar smell about it. It got more and more peculiar until Mrs Schlotsheimer figured out there was something about my raincoat. She brought the coat out in front of the class and asked, Whose is it?

Mine, I said.

continued on next page.

The **Oh My God Fart**

PART II
continued from previous page.

I might have known, Mrs. Schlotsheimer said.

Then she made the mistake of sticking her hand into the raincoat pocket. I cannot imagine why she should have wanted to do this, but she did. And I guess her hand broke the egg, because you would not believe the terrible smell, like a poisonous gas, a heavy cloud, that filled the classroom then. Several kids around the room started looking sick. It was the most absolutely rotten smell I have ever smelled.

Oh, shit, Mrs. Schlotsheimer said.

And then she pulled her hand back out of the coat pocket and said, oh my God.

She said that several times over.

Since I have tried to keep this work as clean as possible considering the subject matter, I have identified this most awful and dreadful stinking of all farts—a fart that smells like a month-old rotten egg—as the Oh My God Fart. If you should ever encounter it, however, you may first want to say, oh shit, in the same spirit as poor Mrs. Schlotsheimer. Which would be understandable.

The **Omen Fart**

This is the adult version of the Poo-Poo Fart (from my previous book.) About the only difference is that the farter will not say anything. He will just look kind of funny and head for the john. This one is easy to spot if you pay attention.

The **Pacifist Fart**

This is a fart by a person who has been farted on by a Yuppie (see under Y, the Yuppie Fart). Instead of punching out the Yuppie he waits until he gets the Yuppie in an elevator or a compact car and then he cuts one that has the Yuppie barfing. But there has been no violence.

P

The **Peaceful Fart**

A very private fart, soft and easy and slow. It occurs just before you are going to sleep. It sounds almost like a lullaby. I am thinking particularly of the lullaby that goes, "Blow, blow, wind of the western sea," if you know that one.

The **Pisces Fart**

The Pisces Fart is the most rank and rotten
sign-of-the-Zodiac fart there is. This is because
Pisces is pretty close to feces.
And that's pretty close to a pun.

The **Political Fart**

A very unusual fart, pecular to politicians. While it is both a loud and long fart, it has, surprisingly, no real identifiable odor. More often than not it has no odor at all. He has shot a blank, so to speak. But while there is nothing to it, at the time it will somehow draw a crowd. Even applause. It is ridiculous.

The **Port-a-Potty Fart**

No one likes to fart in a port-a-potty, but sometimes it cannot be avoided. Sometimes that is all that happens; a bunch of farts. Farting in a port-a-potty is like farting in a barrel; it can sound like thunder. Several good Port-a-Potty Farts in a row can bring pedestrian traffic to a halt in all directions. There can be cheers when you open the door and step out. The only thing more embarrassing than a loud fart in a port-a-potty is a splash so loud it sounds like you fell in.

Q

The **Quiver Fart**

A group one identification fart only.
When you fart, it quivers. If it tickles then
it is the Tickle Fart. If you have to scratch
it then it is the Scratchass Fart.

The **Reluctant Fart**

This is a fart that has really been around for awhile. It is probably one of the oldest farts known to man. (See Montaigne, quoted elsewhere in this work.) The Reluctant Fart is a fart that seems to have a mind of its own. It gives the impression that it likes staying where it is. It will come when it is ready, not before. This can take half a day in some instances. My mother says it was that way with me about getting born. I was in no big hurry. Neither is the Reluctant Fart. When it is finally farted it is way past due. According to my mother I was way past due by about a month. This may be one of the reasons my father sometimes refers to me as, "You little fart." Although he probably has better reasons than that.

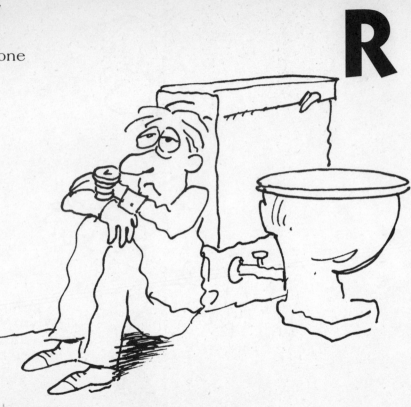

The **Republican Fart**

This is a fart that tells you by its odor alone that it was farted by a wealthy man. It is strictly a red meat fart and no doubt about it. A fart like this in a poor neighborhood could cause some bitterness.

If you are a Democrat you will know immediately that you simply have not got what it takes for this one. Which you can figure is maybe one good thing about being poor and a Democrat, as who wants to live with farts like that on their conscience?

The **Sandpaper Fart**

This one scratches. Otherwise it may not amount to much. As a group one identification it is hard to miss. You may wonder if there is more to it than just some gas. Otherwise, what is it that scratches? There is still much that is not known about farts.

You should remember that if you reach back and scratch, it automatically becomes a Scratchass Fart. So if you need this one for your list, don't scratch. Common.

The **Sinner's Fart**

This is just a different name for the S.B.D. Fart and should not be listed separately, in my opinion. Still, some people like the idea that bad people fart worse farts than good people. So if you like to think something like this is true, I suppose it is up to you. Common with people who think like this.

The **Smirk Fart**

Another name for the Jerk Fart.
Most jerks smirk when they fart.

The **Somebody's Aunt Fart**

Which is a strange name for a fart, all right. But the lady who farts this fart is always named Aunt Jane or Aunt Rose or Aunt Sue and is always old and somewhat deaf. She will walk across a room farting a neat little string of farts, one with every step. It would be cool if she did it on purpose, but she doesn't even know she has farted. It is hard not to laugh, even if it is your own aunt.

The **Splatter Fart**

Unfortunately the Splatter Fart exists.
It is the wettest of all farts.
It probably should not be called a fart at all.
A group one identification only.
And you better hope not.

The **Stuck Elevator Fart**

It is a good thing that the Stuck Elevator Fart is as rare as it is, as it is the one fart that can truly make you wonder if you are going to die. It only happens when the elevator gets stuck, of course, but it will happen then for certain. I have done considerable research on this, and I do not know of a single time that an elevator got stuck and nobody farted before it got unstuck. Naturally you get scared in a stuck elevator, and that doesn't help a person not to fart. If there is not already a panic in a stuck elevator, there will be one for sure when the Stuck Elevator Farts start getting farted. You will think you are choking or being strangled or being poisoned by gas. If the elevator is dark as well it can be terrifying. "What a terrible way to die," you will think. And it would be.

The **Subversive Fart**

If you fart while singing "God Bless America" or the National Anthem, or while saluting the flag, you have farted the Subversive Fart. This is true even if it was an accident. If you did it on purpose this is more serious, of course. If you were to make a point of doing this as a regular thing it could probably get you into trouble with certain people, or even the government. However, it seems to me that if that is your point of view you are entitled to it. Some people would stop you from farting on Sunday if they could.

The **Sweet Fart**

This is one of the most disgusting farts there is. Even when it is your own you cannot stand it. It smells exactly like Juicy Fruit, only worse. Sweeter. When this is a group two fart it is best not to try and identify the farter, particularly if he or she is a friend of the opposite sex, as the Sweet Fart can cool things between two people in a hurry.

Maybe forever.

The **Taco Bell Fart**

T

The Taco Bell Fart is far richer and full-bodied than your ordinary Junk Fart and takes longer to build up. Sometimes hours or even a day. But it will get there. And it will hang around after, too, even on a windy day.

The **Tap Dancing Fart**

I have always had the feeling that tap dancing and farting go together. I believe I read something to this effect by Mr. Kurt Vonnegut. He wrote about some people on another planet who communicated by tap dancing and farting. A real neat planet, for sure, and a great story. But anyhow, the Tap Dancing Fart I am talking about here is meant to be a concealed fart. A person feels a fart coming on and starts tap dancing like crazy, hoping no one will hear their fart. It almost never works. People know something is wrong and wait to see what it is. And when it is over they say, "Oh, I see, a Tap Dancing Fart."

The **Tapioca Fart**

The Tapioca Fart comes from eating tapioca pudding. It is as though half of those little slimy fish-eye pellets in the pudding—like little guppy eyes—turn into farts. Then they come slipping out like BB's through a funnel. There is little doubt that the Tapioca Fart has far more notes per fart than any other multiple-noted fart, although the notes are all as tiny as hummingbird farts, if there is such a thing.

The **Telephone Fart**

This is a fart that happens while you are talking on the telephone. If it is not a real boomer you can probably get away with it, unless you are one of those people who cannot fart and talk at the same time, in which case the pause may make the other person suspicious. "Did you fart?" they may ask. You can deny it if you want to, I suppose.

However, it is hard to get away with a Telephone Fart if a friend comes into the room right after you have farted. You cannot lead him clear of the fart because you are still talking on the phone. He will walk right into it. Naturally he will know it was you, although you can try putting your hand over the phone and telling your friend that it was that fellow you were talking to that farted. Your friend will either laugh or, if he is real durnb, he may believe you. Either way, you have made the best of it.

The Telephone Fart is a common fart, and generally one of the safer ones; but not always.

The **Television Fart**

There is a bunch of people sitting around eating popcorn and watching TV and somebody farts. But nobody says anything. Nobody even looks around, as rank as the fart may be. The only sign they give is that for awhile they all stop eating popcorn. This shows what a terrible hold television has on people, I guess.

The **Thank God I'm Alone Fart**

Everyone knows this rotten fart. You look around after you have farted and say, Thank God I'm alone. Then you get out of there. If it has to happen though, that is the best way for it to happen. Like finding out that your fly is unzipped. You should be alone.

The **Traffic Jam Fart**

You are riding along in an automobile and you roll down the window so that the wind can blow away the fart you are about to fart, and just as you lean to one side and lift up a little to let the fart out, you are suddenly stopped in a traffic jam. And there is nothing you can do but sit there in your own rotten fart. Maybe you can blow your horn, but it won't help much. This is a surprisingly common fart.

The **Thunder Mug Fart**

An unusual fart because the only true Thunder Mug Fart has to be farted into one of those old heavy china thunder mugs, which is where the name came from. A port-a-pottie or your regular john does not give the same effect at all. A Thunder Mug Fart really thunders. Uncommon due to the fact that old fashioned thunder mugs are uncommon.

The **Thus Spake Zarathustra Fart**

This fart is similar, in a way, to the Did An Angel Speak Fart, which occurs around religious people, when one of them farts and someone says, "Did an angel speak?" Only this one happens around intellectuals. Unsually professors. One professor will fart and another one will say, "Thus spake Zarathustra." A little humor there. Then they will go back to arguing. To get this one on your list you should know who Nietzsche is, or at least who Zarathustra was.

The **Tickle Fart**

A group one only and one of the easiest to identify. It tickles. Usually a slow soft sort of fart. If you like being tickled this is the fart for you. Personally, it is no favorite of mine. I do not like being tickled. Even if I did, that is not where I would want to be tickled.

The **Truck Driver Fart**

It is not nice to characterize an entire occupation through the grossness of the farts of some of its members, but in this instance I can see no way around it. If what my uncle says is true—and he used to be a truck driver—truck driver farts are in a class by themselves. No group of people anywhere, he says, fart more, or worse, farts than do truck drivers. The reason for this, he says, is because of the rotten food at all those truckstops. Truck drivers only eat at truckstops, he says, because that is the only place where there is room for them to park their trucks.

My uncle had been drinking some when we spoke of these matters, but I have the feeling that he spoke the truth.

(See also under B, the Broccoli Fart.) This is the real thing. It comes from eating a bunch of broccoli in the first place and is unavoidable. If you really like broccoli, and are otherwise strange, this is a fart that could make you drool.

The **Underwear Ripper**

Sound alone is diagnostic with this fart. It will usually happen when the person is sitting down. It is one of the longer farts. It will sound so much like a piece of cloth being ripped that it can fool a person sitting in the next room. Naturally it will not fool the farter. He will know he has not ripped his underwear. But right then he may not be too sure about anything else.

The **Vertigo Fart**

V

Things will seem strange at the time and for some time after to the person who has farted a Vertigo Fart. This is the only fart known to make a person actually dizzy. It has been said that even people just standing around can be made dizzy by this fart, but I do not know if this is so or not. I have never been around when it happened. Generally a group one identification; if you fart and get dizzy, that's it.

The **Waterbed Fart**

With the Waterbed Fart, if you happen to have a good deal of gas, you can sort of rock yourself to sleep with farts. Or so I am told. I have never slept on a waterbed or had all that much gas. The thing is, the force of the farts gets the waterbed kind of gently rocking. That is what I am told, anyhow, and it may be true. Seems to me, though, that they would have to be pretty powerful farts. Farts that powerful would probably keep you awake just from the noise.

The Who Cut the Cheeze Fart

An easy identification with this one. Someone has got to say, Who cut the cheeze? when the fart is first noticed or it cannot be called a Who Cut the Cheeze Fart. It may or may not have an odor like strong cheese, but it will have an odor.

The Winnie Fart

This is the only fart in this work named after a person. I do not know Winnie personally. Only by reputation. She is a grandmother and is pretty deaf. Actually, she is deaf as a post. And she farts a lot. She is also a great talker. It is said of her that she will be talking away a mile a minute and will fart a fart that blows pictures off the wall and moves the furniture around and still never miss a word. She won't even know she has farted. At least that is what they say. I believe she really knows, however. I imagine she just doesn't give a damn.

If you do not wish to call this the Winnie Fart you can call it the Grandmother Fart, but in my book, and this is my book, it is the Winnie Fart, and a great one.

X

The **Xylophone Fart**

I am not really positive there is a Xylophone Fart. I have never heard one myself. I have put it in as a possible fart subject to verification. This way I will have two farts starting with the letter X (see my previous book for the other one). If you will look in a dictionary you will see that there are not too many words in the whole English language that begin with the letter X. So the two X farts will have to do.

However, this gives your real fart freak something to shoot for. Who will be the first to positively identify a Xylophone Fart? Time will tell.

The **Yak Fart**

y

The yak is a wild ox with long shaggy hair and enormous horns who stands six feet tall at the shoulder. If you look at a picture of a yak you will get the feeling that this is the beast that could fart one powerful fart. I am sorry that this book does not include animal farts, as the Yak Fart would really be a great one. However, a Yak Fart by a person would probably be fatal, so unless you are a sadist or really morbid you should not go around hoping to get one of these on your list.

The **Yodel Fart**

The Yodel Fart sounds like a fart whose voice is changing, or like a yodel. It can be either a Swiss mountain yodeler type of yodel or an American cowboy singer type of yodel. Either one will do. Not so rare as the Xylophone Fart, but just about.

The **Yo-Yo Fart**

This is a spectacular fart. A real dilly. Sound alone identifies it. I makes the Octave Fart sound like a hiccough. It starts out on the highest fart note possible and goes all the way down to the lowest fart note possible. And then to the amazement of everyone it comes all the way back up again. Extremely rare.

The **Yuppie Fart**

The person who farts this fart will wear a shirt with an alligator on it and will get in front of you before he farts. There is nothing great about this fart at all. You will probably not think too much of the farter, either. Strictly group two.

The **Zodiac Fart**

When people ask my father what is his astrological sign he will say, "Vertigo or feces, I forget which." This does not usually get a laugh but he will say it anyhow. The Zodiac Fart is a fart that begins with the letter Z. Further description would no doubt prove redundant. If you believe in the Zodiac Fart you probably think the world is flat, too.